Joy Church
P.O. Box 247
Mount Juliet, TN 37121
www.joychurch.net

Printed in the United States of America

Publisher's Cataloging-in-Publication data
Frease, Jim.
Winning with Wisdom: Pearls of Wisdom for Your Next Right Decision
- Volume One / Jim Frease.
p. 196
ISBN 978-0-9983918-0-9
1. Motivational 2. Inspirational. 3. Christian Living.

First Edition
First Printing 2016 / Second Printing 2017

WINNING WITH
WISDOM

PEARLS OF WISDOM FOR YOUR
NEXT RIGHT DECISION

Winning with Wisdom

Wisdom is the principal thing.
Therefore, get wisdom.

The Bible tells us, "Wise men store up knowledge..." (Proverbs 10:14 NKJV). Did you know the quality of your life is determined by the quality of your decisions, and the quality of your decisions is determined by the quality of information you "store" up? Therefore, if we truly desire a better quality of life, we must make better quality decisions with better quality information.

This little "nugget" style book is designed to invest in your storehouse of knowledge so you can eventually enjoy a better quality of life. As you peruse through the pages of this book, don't be overwhelmed by the quantity of information, but rather focus in on the quality of change.

Remember this: invest in knowledge now, and it will compound in wisdom later!

You are not a loser; you are a "chooser"! *Winning with Wisdom* is designed to help you make your next right decision.

- JIM FREASE

life is CONNECTED!

THE CHOICES YOU MAKE TODAY DIRECTLY AFFECT YOUR TOMORROW.

Table of contents

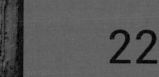

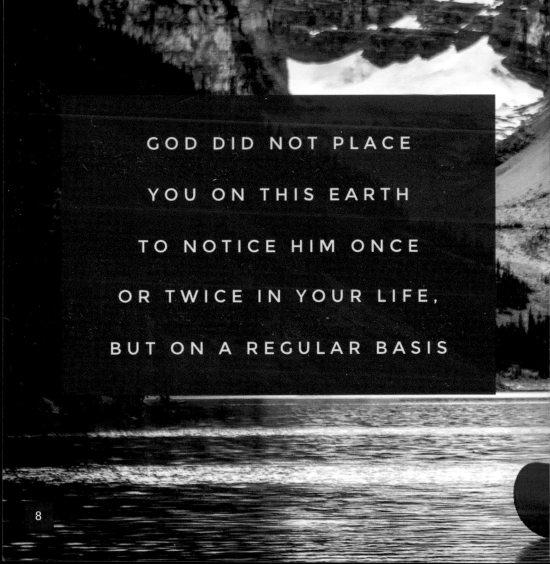

GOD DID NOT PLACE
YOU ON THIS EARTH
TO NOTICE HIM ONCE
OR TWICE IN YOUR LIFE,
BUT ON A REGULAR BASIS

RELATIONSHIP
WITH GOD

God does not love you
based on what you've done,
but based on what He's done.

God does not love you based on who you are;
God loves you based on who He is!

Love is not based
on the character of the receiver,
it's based on the
character of the Giver.

GOD LOVES YOU
AS IF YOU ARE
THE ONLY PERSON
IN THIS WORLD
TO LOVE.

Your God is a watching, loving, running, hugging, and kissing God
(Luke 15:11-32).

How you view Him will determine how much you come to Him.

How you view Him will determine your outlook on life.

GOD IS NOT A CAR-WRECKING,
CANCER-CAUSING
CREATOR,
BUT A LOVING,
LIFE-GIVING LORD.

If you give God the first part of your day,
you will act on life instead of reacting to life.

Don't struggle to find God's will,
but continually seek Him
and believe He is leading you into His will!

God is not looking for your ability,
but your availability.

When God's Word becomes
the main part of your prayer life,
you start with the solution
instead of the problem.

Bending your will away *from*
God and His Word is called stubbornness;
Bending your will *toward*
God and His Word is called determination.

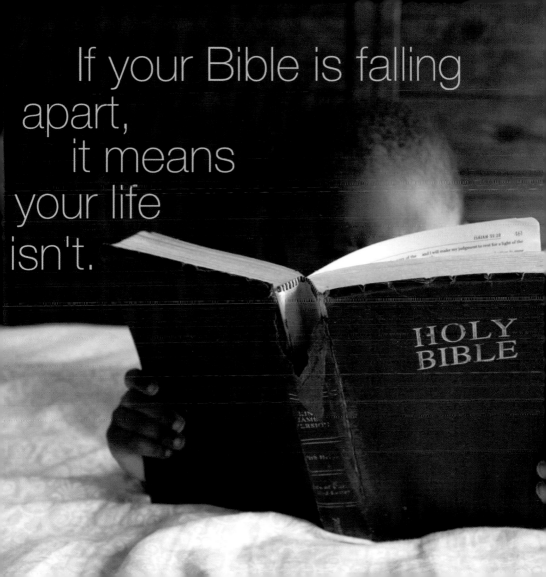

The very knowledge that Jesus
continues to love and enjoy us
as we are maturing
is the foundational truth
that empowers us to mature.

Understanding His passion for you
will ignite your passion for Him.

GOD DOESN'T JUST HAVE LOVE -

HE IS LOVE!

You are always comfortable
in the presence of those who love you.

God's love doesn't say,
"I will love you if…"
God's love says,
"I will love you, period."

God will never love you more
than He does now!

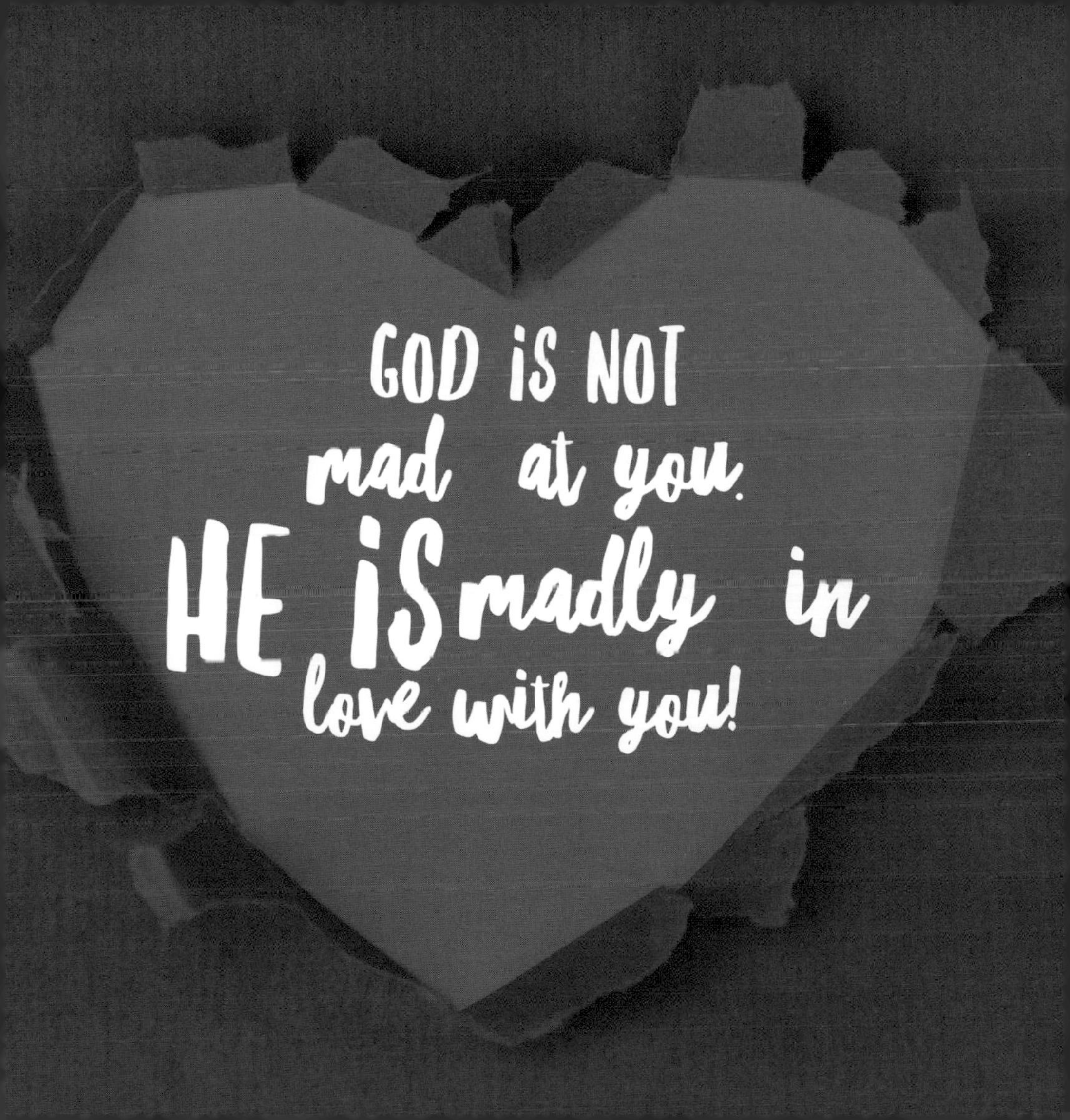
GOD iS NOT
mad at you.
HE iS madly in
love with you!

SOMETIMES AGE

AND MATURITY

COME TOGETHER.

SOMETIMES AGE COMES

ALL BY ITSELF.

CHARACTER

Talent is a gift,
but character is a choice.

Ability is useless
without the discipline to point it
in the right direction.

When it comes to your character,
work on your weaknesses.
When it comes to your gifts,
work on your strengths.

YOUR GIFT CAN ONLY TAKE YOU

AS FAR AS YOUR CHARACTER CAN KEEP YOU.

What you do
when no one is watching
determines who you are
when everyone is watching.

Integrity always chooses
people over things,
principle over convenience,
discretion over immediacy,
and character over personal gain.

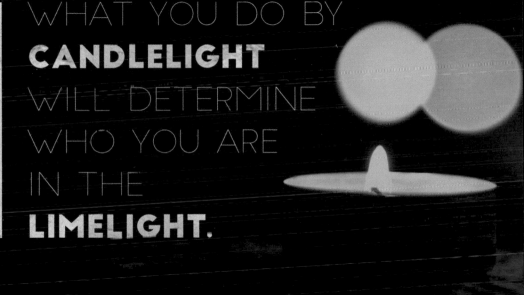

WHAT YOU DO BY **CANDLELIGHT** WILL DETERMINE WHO YOU ARE IN THE **LIMELIGHT.**

Self-pity says, "Why me?"
Overcomers say, "Why not me?"

Crisis does not create character;
it reveals it.

If you had a bad start
to your day or your life,
simply finish strong
(Ecclesiastes 7:8).

LEARN TO MAKE
RIGHT DECISIONS
IN THE MIDST OF
WRONG CIRCUMSTANCES.

Many times, people don't want to confront
what they still secretly enjoy.

Crossing a line,
whether it be by an inch or a mile,
is still out of bounds.

When you tell God about it
is not when He finds out about it.

ANYTHING YOU HAVE TO HIDE TO DO

is wrong TO YOU.

You can stand tall in principle
and still stand by people.

Beware of the "everybody is doing it"
or "nobody is doing it" syndrome.

If you refuse to compromise,
you'll be rejected by many
but promoted by *One*.

We must do all we can to reach people,
except compromise.

NEVER COMPROMISE ON PRINCIPLE.
FREQUENTLY COMPROMISE ON PREFERENCE.

Personality is who you are in public.
Character is who you are in private.

When you are small, you must build
the right things into your system,
or the big will kill you!

Commitment is sustained by character.

Talent is a gift, but character is a choice.

CHARACTER, NOT SKILL, IS THE KEY TO BEING USED BY GOD.

It's not the sin
you struggle with that kills you;
it's the sin you tolerate.

People tend to condemn in others
what they allow in themselves.

Kill sin while it's little,
or it will grow up to enslave you.

SIN WILL TAKE YOU FARTHER

THAN YOU WANT TO GO,

KEEP YOU LONGER

THAN YOU WANT TO STAY,

AND COST YOU MORE

THAN YOU WANT TO PAY!

Character is revealed in conflict.

Don't hide behind your gift
as an excuse for not developing your character.

God is far more interested in what you're
becoming than what you're doing!

A MAN'S CHARACTER IS ALWAYS

MORE IMPORTANT THAN HIS GIFT

(PSALM 26:11)

You must quit living by
what you have done,
and instead start living
by what He has done.

The flesh trying to clean up the flesh
is much like using a tornado
to clean up a hurricane
—it's only going to make a bigger mess.

WHEN YOU MESS UP,
FESS UP
DON'T COVER UP.

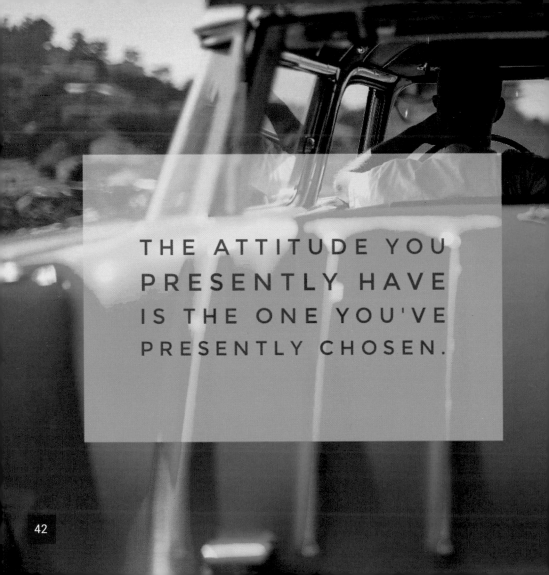

THE ATTITUDE YOU
PRESENTLY HAVE
IS THE ONE YOU'VE
PRESENTLY CHOSEN.

ATTITUDE

People meet your attitude
before they meet you.

Attitude is doing the will of God
with a smile.

Never let others determine your attitude.

All bad attitudes
have their roots in selfishness.

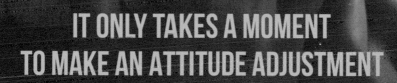

IT ONLY TAKES A MOMENT
TO MAKE AN ATTITUDE ADJUSTMENT

In life, you have a choice:
You can get bitter, or you can get better.
You can be a victim, or you can be a victor.

Your attitude will determine
your altitude.

Attitude can give us
an uncommonly positive perspective.

IT'S EASY TO LAUGH

WHEN EVERYTHING IS GOING RIGHT.

IT'S IMPORTANT TO LAUGH

WHEN EVERYTHING IS GOING WRONG.

You must take responsibility for your attitude.

Speaking what you know
will eventually change how you feel.

Look at life from your position,
not your condition.

Only two people will show up
to your pity party:
you and the devil.

ARGUE FOR YOUR LIMITATIONS AND SURE ENOUGH, THEY WILL LIMIT YOU.

Excusers are losers.

Moaners are loners.

Grumblers are fumblers.

Whiners are not winners.

Complainers are not obtainers.

Pitiful is not powerful.

Gripers get the vipers.

YOU CAN NEVER BLAME
your way to success

Your future will always
look a little brighter
with the right attitude.

With time comes clarity.
With clarity comes perspective.
With perspective comes
better decisions.

NEVER MAKE A

LIFE-CHANGING DECISION

FROM A VALLEY.

CHANGE YOUR ATTITUDE

IN A VALLEY

AND CHANGE DIRECTION

FROM A PEAK.

Hidden attitudes will eventually
find their way into your heart,
and what's in your heart
will eventually find its way into your mouth.

Attitude draws people to us.
Attitude repels people from us.

You can't always choose
the people or circumstances in your life,
but you can always choose
your attitude toward them.

IT'S NOT THE FACTS, FEARS AND FOLKS YOU FACE, BUT HOW YOU FACE THE FACTS, FEARS AND FOLKS! ATTITUDE IS EVERYTHING.

Life is 10% what happens to you
and 90% how you respond to it.

What gets your attention gets you.

Develop an attitude of gratitude.

There are no negatives
in the Kingdom of God;
only positives waiting to be birthed.

IT'S A CHOICE
TO REJOICE!

PEOPLE NEED YOU TO
GET CLOSER TO JESUS.
JESUS NEEDS YOU TO
GET CLOSER TO PEOPLE.

RELATIONSHIPS

If your relationships are dysfunctional,
your life will be too.

You will always rise or compromise
to the level of your association.

If you want to determine
the value of any relationship,
measure its contribution to *your* victory.
If you want to determine
the value of your relationship to others,
measure your contribution to *their* victory.

The most powerful people are empowering people.

If you can't serve the people, you can't teach the people.

Hurting people hurt people.
Whole people help people.

PEOPLE-WORK

Always

COMES BEFORE
PAPERWORK

In life, there will always be givers and takers. You cannot have a long-term relationship with a taker.

Trusting character and trusting judgment are two different things.

Love quickly; trust slowly.

TRUST
IN
INCREMENTS

Doing little things for others
makes you happy.

Humble people don't think less of themselves;
they just think of themselves less.

The most important relationships in your life
are built on small, consistent deposits of time.
Consistent, not random availability.

YOU MAKE
A LIVING BY
WHAT YOU GET.
YOU MAKE
A LIFE
BY WHAT
YOU GIVE.

Your friends are either
energizers or expenditures.

Your anointing is for many;
your life is for few.

Never try to get someone to stay
when they are determined to go.

DETERMINING WHICH
RELATIONSHIPS
SHOULD BE INITIATED,
CULTIVATED, OR ELIMINATED
WILL DETERMINE
JUST HOW FAR YOU ARE
ELEVATED

God will use the humanity
of those in authority
to test your promotability.

The quicker you learn to submit
to imperfect vessels,
the quicker you'll be promoted.

Learn to flow with those
who foster your future
(Mark 3:31-35).

Adversity reveals loyalty.

There are two kinds of people:
those who love where you've *been*, and
those who love where you're *going*.

NEVER

DISCUSS YOUR
FUTURE
WITH THOSE
WHO DON'T SEE
THEMSELVES IN IT.

When you are all wrapped up in yourself,
it makes for a very small package.

Don't live your life based on
what other people think of you;
live your life thinking of others.

When you build the dreams of others,
God will build yours!

WITH ONE SMALL EXCEPTION,
THE ENTIRE WORLD'S POPULATION
CONSISTS OF SOMEONE OTHER THAN
YOU.

You will never find peace
in another man's head.

Never try to download from people
what they are not hard-wired to give you.

Many times we are willing
to love others unconditionally—
as long as they meet our conditions.

MISMATCHED
EXPECTATIONS
BREED DISAPPOINTMENT.

People wildly underestimate
the power of the tiniest touch of kindness.

Some of the best time you can spend
is the time you invest in people's lives.

Big people always make you feel
bigger in their presence.

ALWAYS
LEAVE
PEOPLE
Lifted

THREE WAYS TO NEVER BE CRITICIZED:
SAY NOTHING
DO NOTHING
BE NOTHING

LEADERSHIP

The only way to keep leading
is to keep growing.

If you're always
the smartest person in the room,
it's time to find a new room!

The more wisdom you have,
the more you'll be right—
and the less you'll need to be.

Don't be a know-it-all.
Be a learn-it-all.

LEADERS

ARE

LEARNERS

You begin to succeed in life when the successes of others matter to you.

Always lead by love and loyalty, never by fear and intimidation.

Have care-frontation, not confrontation.

The same amount of people you can help is the same amount of people you can hurt.

A WISE LEADER
LEADS WITH
INSPIRATION AND MOTIVATION
RATHER THAN
INTIMIDATION AND MANIPULATION.

If you are a leader that has *followers*,
you'll have limits.
If you are a leader that has *leaders*,
you'll have no limits.

You must be able to focus on
and rally around the team's vision.
Focus will enhance your ability to execute.

If you don't know where you're going,
you'll end up somewhere else.

One of a leader's biggest assignments is to get and give perspective.

The devil has a hard time hiding
in a place called communication.

Assumption is the lowest form
of communication.

Communicate until you
understand each other,
the problem, and the solution.

In communication,
the issue is not who's right,
but making things right.

THE POWER
TO COMMUNICATE IS THE
POWER TO LEAD

The spiritual leader of today
is the one who served in anonymity yesterday.

Your ability to relate to God will give you
the ability to relate to others.

Your character must match
your level of exposure.

You build a team out of relationship,
not out of authority.

EVERYTHING

Rises and falls

TO THE LEVEL
OF LEADERSHIP

There is no traffic on the extra mile.

Be a task finisher,
not a clock watcher.

Leadership begins with
a simple decision to pay the price,
and ends the moment you cease to pay it.

Defend yourself only when it will help others.
Stay silent when it will only help you.

THE PRICE YOU'RE PAYING FOR

LEADERSHIP TODAY

WILL BE THE VALUE OF YOUR

LEADERSHIP TOMORROW

What you allow in moderation,
the people that follow you will do in excess.
They can, but you can't.

Never allow your personal freedom
to become another man's stumbling block.

If you want to impress someone,
tell them your successes.
If you want to impact someone,
tell them your failures.

LEADERSHIP IS INFLUENCE

Leaders who fail to lift people up will,
in the long run, not be lifted up.

You may think you are a leader,
but if no one is following,
you're just out for a walk!

If it's lonely at the top, you're not a leader.
Take someone with you.

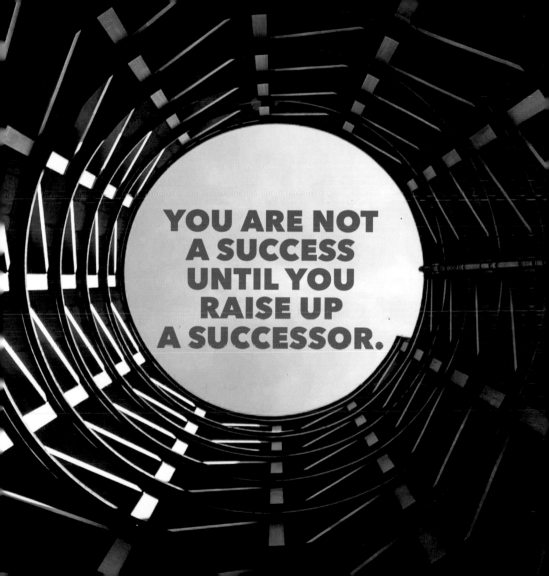

In important decisions,
it's better to be too slow than too fast.
Better to play catch up than clean up!

There is a spiritual momentum
to every divine decision.
Once you know, go.

Character is formed when you
make the tough decisions.

It's not always the most talented team that wins,
but sometimes the most unified.

A team does not compete against each other,
but completes each other.

Strong teams build strong relationships.

Unity is not sounding the same,
but sounding together.

Never try to succeed alone.

TEAMWORK MAKES THE DREAM WORK!

YOUR DESTINY

IS NOT TO BE DECIDED.

YOUR DESTINY

IS TO BE DISCOVERED.

DESTINY

Your intimacy with God
will be the key to your confidence.
If you know what He's saying,
you'll know where you're going.

Intimacy is the goal;
productivity is the result!

It takes constant intimacy and integrity
to finish your destiny.

DESTINY COMES through INTIMACY!

Discipline is the bridge
between goals and accomplishments.
That bridge must be crossed daily.

Discipline is the force that squeezes you
into a narrow place called destiny.

THE TWO GREATEST GAPS IN LIFE
ARE THE GAPS BETWEEN
KNOWING AND DOING,
AND WANTING AND HAVING.
CLOSE THE FIRST GAP AND THE
SECOND WILL AUTOMATICALLY CLOSE.

Your consistent choices
formulate your character,
and from your character,
you create your choices.

The role you continually play
will be the role you eventually become.

You don't decide your future.
You decide your habits,
and your habits decide your future.

HABIT WILL ALWAYS TAKE YOU FURTHER THAN DESIRE

Many times, the will of God will initially
take you one step backward
in order to eventually position
you two steps forward.

The reason God won't let you get away
with such low decisions is because
you have such a high calling.

EVERY DECISION YOU MAKE
WILL EITHER TAKE YOU
CLOSER TO OR
FURTHER FROM
YOUR DESTINY

Never let what you did define you.
Never let what was done to you define you.
Always let what Jesus did for you define you.

Emotions that will keep you stuck in the past:
guilt, regret, and self-pity.

If the devil can remind you of your past,
you will always have fear for your future.

YOU'LL NEVER FIND MOTIVATION IN YOUR REAR VIEW MIRROR

Facing difficulties is inevitable;
learning from them is optional.

Learn from your mistakes
so you don't repeat them.

Don't nurse it. Don't rehearse it. Disperse it!

Admit it, quit it, then forget it!

LEARN FROM IT.

LAUGH AT IT.

LET IT GO!

To foster a better future,
you must first become
dissatisfied with the present.

God will not show you
what you are going *through*.
He'll show you what you are going *to*.

The Holy Spirit is the best guide to a successful
future because He's been there before!

ONE OF THE BEST QUESTIONS

YOU CAN ASK GOD IS,

"WHAT IS MY NEXT STEP?"

Pictures of joy release
the power of endurance.

It is your enemy's assignment
to stir up a storm around you
so you don't focus on the seed within you.

Never gaze at what
you don't want in your future.

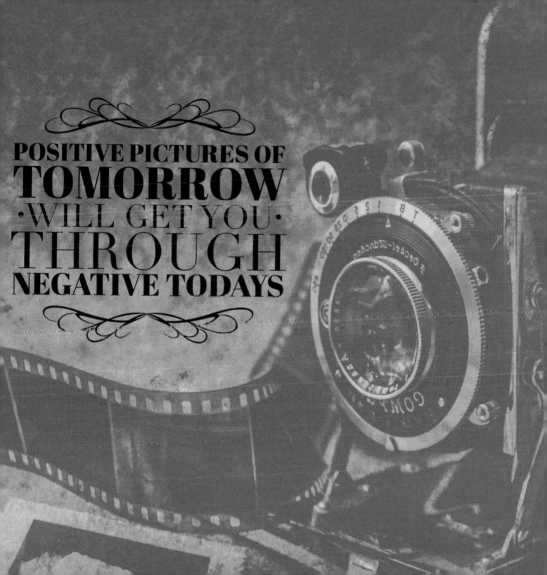

You must change yourself,
but not *by* yourself.

The degree to which
you let God change you
will be the degree to which
you can change your world.

The difference between
a somebody and a nobody
is a somebody was a nobody
who conquered an enemy!

When God plans your future,
He doesn't consult your past.

When you live in the past,
your problems will last.

All fear of the future is based
on a negative of the past.

IN ORDER TO GET TO

A successful future

YOU MUST LET GO OF YOUR PAST

The number one reason people fail
to reach their God-given destiny
is they fail to connect today's decisions
with tomorrow's destiny.

One of the greatest mistakes
you can make in life
is continually fearing
you will make one.

LIFE IS SIMPLY A SERIES OF **MAKING THE** NEXT RIGHT DECISION.

You will never find new levels of fruitfulness without new levels of faithfulness.

You will never find new levels of influence without new levels of commitment.

YOU WILL NEVER DISCOVER

Uncharted waters

UNTIL YOU ARE WILLING
TO LOSE SIGHT OF THE SHORE

When the real is less than ideal,
don't throw away the ideal.
If your real is less than ideal,
God has a plan for wherever you land.

If you will prioritize the Word,
it will help you prioritize your life.

GOD HAS
A WONDERFUL PLAN FOR YOUR LIFE,
JUST NOT A WONDERFUL
LIFE FOR YOUR PLAN!

Your job is what you do;
your work is what you were born to do.

Your prosperity is not in your job;
it's in your work.

Your work flows from your gift.

Find your gift, refine your gift,
and then people will find your gift!

YOUR JOB IS
A CAREER.
YOUR WORK IS
A CALLING.

A passionate person
doesn't need to push himself to start;
he has to force himself to stop.

Purpose breeds passion;
passion impacts people.

Passion makes the journey
as enjoyable as the destination.

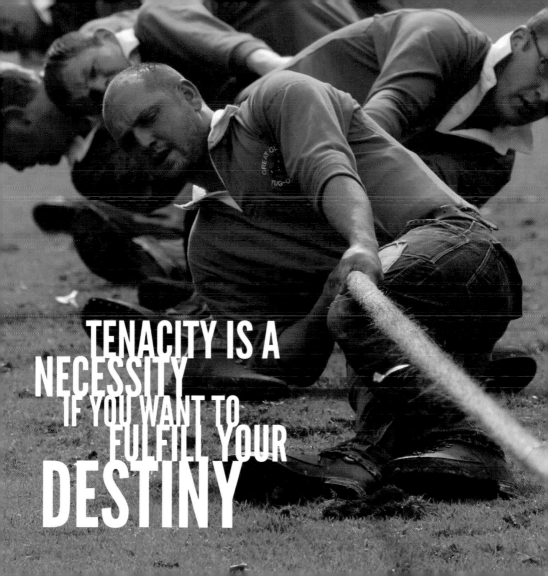

YOUR SUCCESS IS NOT
DETERMINED BY
WHAT YOU DO,
BUT WHETHER OR NOT
YOU'VE DONE WHAT GOD
ASKED YOU TO
DO WHEN HE
ASKED YOU TO DO IT

SUCCESS

Who you are today is determined by the
decisions you make,
the actions you take,
and the words you speak.

Don't use your words to describe your life;
use your words to design your life.

YOU ARE NOT

A LOSER.

YOU ARE A

CHOOSER.

Real champions are not made by
what we do when people are watching,
but the life we live when no one sees.

Unsuccessful people try to hang on
to a season even after it's over.
Successful people learn
from every past season
and then embrace the new.

IT'S HARD TO BOARD

The Plane Of Success

WHEN YOU HAVE
TOO MUCH
"CARRY-ON BAGGAGE"

You can get anywhere you want to go as long as you're willing to take enough small steps.

In order for you to enter your future successfully, it must be revealed to you progressively.

You will never progress beyond your last point of disobedience.

If you are not receiving your next step, go back and do what He last told you to do.

GOD ORDERS OUR STEPS,
NOT OUR STRAINS.

Tragedy is an event,
not a lifetime.

Get out of the boat of indecision,
and walk on the water with Him!

Yesterday ended last night.

Don't make failure an excuse
to not try again.

YOU ARE →EITHER← MAKING EXCUSES OR PROGRESS, BUT NOT BOTH.

Motivation gets you going.
Discipline keeps you going.

The price of excellence is discipline.
The cost of mediocrity is disappointment.

Small disciplines repeated
with consistency every day
can lead to great achievements over time.

DISCIPLINE
IS SIMPLY
DOING
WHAT
YOU DON'T
LIKE
SO YOU
CAN HAVE
WHAT YOU
DO LIKE.

Your focus will determine your future.

Passion gives you fire.
Vision gives you focus.

What you continually behold,
you will eventually become!

What you continually view,
you will eventually pursue.

THE ROOT OF ALL FAILURE IS BROKEN FOCUS

Having problems doesn't make you special,
but choosing to face and overcome them does!

The best problem solving
happens before problems happen!

If you look at your problem as special,
it will be especially hard to overcome.

Learn to see the possibility in every problem.

MANY TIMES PEOPLE ARE MORE COMFORTABLE WITH OLD PROBLEMS THAN NEW SOLUTIONS

You can't win from a losing position.

Victory comes to those who stubbornly believe
the Word even when all hell breaks loose!

Victory is simply getting up
one more time than you've fallen.

The bigger the giant,
the bigger the victory.

Be as serious about your victory as the devil is about your defeat.

A successful life is
not determined by self-effort,
but Spirit-empowerment.

Champions are simply those
who put their God-given dreams
above their man-made fears.

You will never quit your way to success.

If you're a problem solver,
God will promote you.

If you're a problem pointer,
you will stop your promotion.

If you're a problem creator,
you'll be demoted!

Your existence is proof that God saw a problem
nobody could solve—but you.

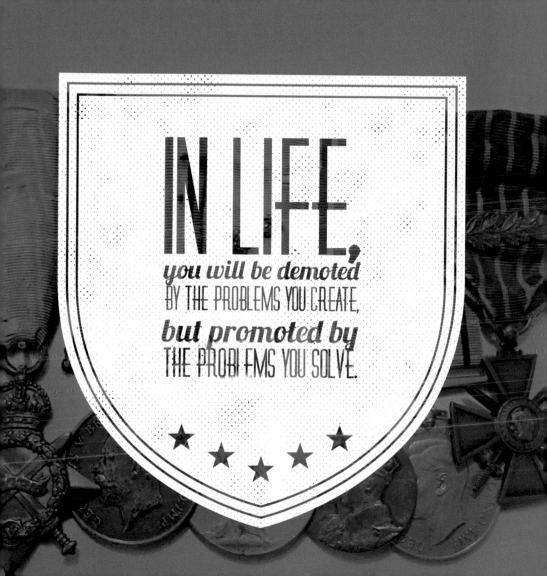

IN LIFE,
you will be demoted
BY THE PROBLEMS YOU CREATE,
but promoted by
THE PROBLEMS YOU SOLVE.

Winners persist through
time, failure, criticism, and rejection.

One thing survivors and winners
have in common:
they don't wallow in the
"why me?" syndrome.

The man who excuses his way out
can always find a thousand exits.

LOSERS MAKE EXCUSES.

WINNERS MAKE PROGRESS!

When you do small things,
always think of big things.
Then small things will become
meaningful things.

Your best guarantee for a great tomorrow
is a good today.

Your faithfulness today
qualifies you for a better tomorrow.
Your unfaithfulness today
disqualifies you from a better tomorrow.

If you don't like the present you're walking in,
start sowing different seeds.

The key to victory is to continue
to do the things you know to do,
even with no apparent
difference in circumstances!

Observe successful lives,
and success secrets will emerge.

Mentors are shortcuts.

IF YOU'RE DOING THE

right things

TODAY,

~~~~~~

YOU ARE ALREADY

A SUCCESS

WAITING TO SHOW UP.

You may never be able
to go back and start again,
but you can start now
and make a new end!

Always get ahold of yourself
before you get ahold of your circumstances.

YOUR OUTWARD CIRCUMSTANCES

WILL NEVER OUTPERFORM

YOUR INWARD PORTRAIT

Sometimes, the biggest enemy
to a successful future is an unsuccessful past.
At other times, it is a successful past.

Greatness is not the absence of weaknesses,
but the recognition of them.

To do anything with excellence,
you must first be prepared to do it poorly.

Success is not a "destination" thing;
it is a "daily basis" thing.

You have to make the decisions
that match the size of your visions.
Many times, people have big visions,
yet they make small decisions.

Make destiny's daily decision—
do the next right thing.

SUCCESSFUL PEOPLE DO

DAILY

WHAT UNSUCCESSFUL PEOPLE DO

OCCASIONALLY

In every battle that you face,
you must learn to pray the promise,
not the problem.

Don't tell God about your big problem;
tell your problem about your big God!

When the storms of life come,
never try to get ahold of your problem;
get ahold of you.

If you're anointed to see the problem,
you're anointed to solve it.

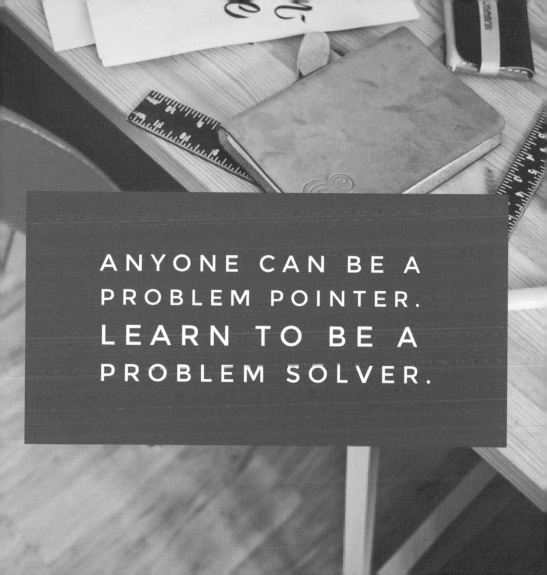

ANYONE CAN BE A
PROBLEM POINTER.
LEARN TO BE A
PROBLEM SOLVER.

If a man hangs on to his way of doing things,
he will be a loser.
If he does things God's way, eventually,
he will be a winner.

If you've fallen, pick something up
while you're down there.

It's easier to go from failure to success
than excuse to success.

FAILING IS AN ACT.
Failure is an attitude.

There is never a perfect time to do anything,
but there is always a time to start.

Stop meditating on the flaws,
and start meditating on the treasure.

Your end can be better than your beginning!

Failure is
the
opportunity
to begin
again
more
intelligently.

Being average is to return no interest
on God's investment in you.

Being average is to pass one's life away with time
rather than pass one's time away with life.

Average is the top of the bottom,
the best of the worst,
the bottom of the top,
and the worst of the best!

AVERAGE IS A
DIRTY WORD

Let another man's pain be your wisdom.

Surround yourself with people
who help you see your objectives,
not just your obstacles.

Don't just look at achievers;
learn from achievers.

THERE ARE THREE WAYS TO LEARN:

FROM YOUR MISTAKES (GOOD)
FROM OTHERS' MISTAKES (BETTER)
FROM OTHERS' SUCCESSES (BEST)

In crises, the first thing out of your mouth
will either set your miracle in motion
or your mess in motion.

Take the faith in your heart
and overcome the doubt in your head
by speaking the Word from your mouth.

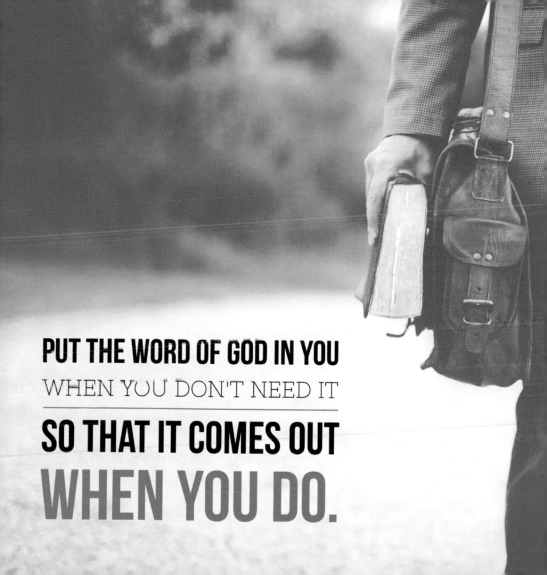

PUT THE WORD OF GOD IN YOU
WHEN YOU DON'T NEED IT
SO THAT IT COMES OUT
WHEN YOU DO.

Meditate on the promises of God until they become larger than life.

The input of God's Word will always bring the output of a changed life.

Wisdom is the ability to interpret life through the eyes of God.

Viewing life through His vantage point will always be our advantage point.

FIND OUT WHAT THE BIBLE SAYS, DO IT FIRST, AND THE BLESSINGS OF GOD WILL ENTER THAT AREA OF YOUR LIFE.

You may say you are
expecting a better tomorrow,
but are you preparing for it today?

Passion is revealed in pursuit.
Expectation is revealed in preparation.

Without preparation,
you'll never meet your destination.

PREPARATION TIME
IS NEVER
WASTED TIME

Memory is for replays;
imagination is for pre-plays.

Anyone who wants to realize their dream
must first wake up.

Cherish your yesterdays.
Dream your tomorrows.
Live your todays.

You make peace with your past
by owning a piece of your past.

Let your past remind you,
but don't let your past define you.

Remember God's past faithfulness
to stir up future triumph.

FOCUS ON HOW FAR YOU'VE COME, NOT HOW FAR YOU NEED TO GO.

The tragedy of life is not that it ends so soon,
but that we wait so long to begin.

How you live your life today will determine
what others say at your funeral later.

Everyone knows they are going to die,
but few actually believe it.
If we did, we would do things differently today.

You'll never have a second chance
to enjoy your today.

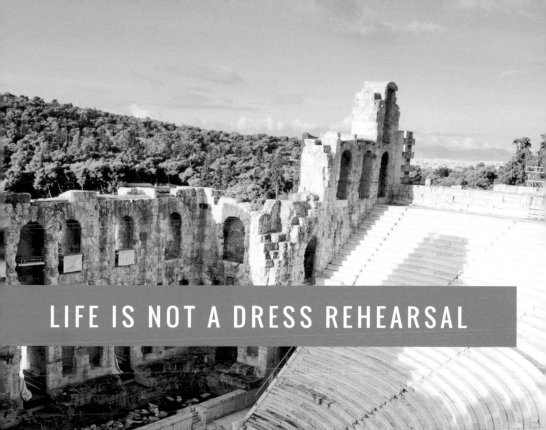

LIFE IS NOT A DRESS REHEARSAL

Life is like a roll of toilet paper—
the older you get, the faster it goes.

Learn to plant trees you'll never sit under.

Life is like jumping
out of an airplane with a parachute:
you've got to get it right the first time.

HOW TO START THE MOST IMPORTANT RELATIONSHIP OF YOUR LIFE

Shark fishing is my hobby. I use a kayak to paddle my bait hundreds of yards into the ocean. I then paddle back and fish from off the shore. A while back, I was in the midst of a four-hour battle with a very large shark. A crowd had gathered from around the beach to see what I was going to reel in! A man in the crowd struck up a conversation with me while I was battling this shark. He asked me what I did for a living and I told him I was a pastor. When people discover that I am a pastor, I get a wide variety of responses.

This man's response was unusual. He simply blurted out with disdain, "Well I hate organized religion!" You could visibly tell he was not expecting the response I gave him back. "Me too", I replied. He was very surprised by my comments so I went further. "You know who else hates organized religion?" I asked. Before he could even respond I shocked him further and said, "Jesus!" Now I had this fellow's undivided attention and I hope I now have yours as well!

You see, Christianity is not about religion it is about a relationship with a loving, Heavenly Father through His one Son, Jesus Christ. I believe you have a figurative "homing beacon" placed on the inside of you by the One who created you...God. A spiritual hole, if you will, that can only be filled by God.

I personally understand this as before I entered into this relationship with Jesus, I tried to fill that hole with women, alcohol and fighting. It was all fun for awhile but when the fun was over and the things I tried to fill that vacuum with came crashing down around me... I still had that "homing beacon" on the inside of me. My Heavenly Father gently, patiently and ever so lovingly calling me home.

Maybe you are reading this and you can sense the emptiness on the inside of you and the loving call of your Heavenly Father imploring you to come home. Why not surrender your life to Him and find the joy, peace and purpose you've been looking for all of your life? Why not start the most important relationship of your life! It's so simple but life transforming.

Please pray this prayer with me. Repeat it out loud but mean it from your heart. I discovered a long time ago that when you reach out to God from your heart, He will always reach back to you with His love!

C'mon, pray this simple prayer with me now:

"Father God, I come to you now. Sin, I turn my back on you. Jesus I turn to You now. I believe you died on the cross just for me. I believe you were raised from the dead... just for me. Come into my heart and be my Lord. I surrender my life to you today. I enter into relationship with you today!"

Now if you prayed that prayer, would you please contact us here at Joy Church and let us know you started the most important relationship of your life? We want to respect your privacy and dignity, but we also want to give you some information to help you walk out this new relationship in a life-giving way!

You may email us at mail@joychurchinternational.org or give us a call at 615-773-5252. You may even write to us if you prefer at Joy Church P.O. Box 247 Mount Juliet, TN 37121

If you live in or are visiting the Nashville / Mount Juliet, TN area, we would love to invite you to join us for one of our upcoming services! For more information and/or directions, please visit our website at www.joychurch.net! We look forward to hearing from you!

Please remember that God loves YOU as if you were the ONLY person in this world to love!

Jim Frease is the Founder and Senior Pastor of Joy Church in Mount Juliet, Tennessee, and Founder and President of World Changers Bible Institute (WCBI). He is also the founder of Joy Ministerial Exchange (JME), a ministerial organization designed to impart to pastors from across the country.

Jim emphasizes a relationship with Jesus Christ, not religion; the Word of God, not tradition; and he emphasizes enjoying one's life, not enduring it. He teaches not just what to do, but how.

Jim and his wife Anne have been married since 1990 and deeply love their son, Johnathan. Jim loves spending time with his family, and enjoys Ohio State football, fishing, Ohio State football, fishing, and Ohio State football. Anne loves to shop. Sometimes, they compromise and shop at Bass Pro.

Most importantly, Jim and Anne are deeply in love with the Lord Jesus Christ and are completely committed to His Word. As they minister, they do so with humor & joy (Nehemiah 8:10) and integrity (Psalm 26:11), propelling the listener to a greater intimacy with Jesus.

Tired of enduring life? Start enjoying life!

Based out of Mt. Juliet, Tennessee, Joy Church is a rapidly growing, multi-generational, multicultural church with people from almost every denominational background—including those with no church background at all.

At Joy Church, we don't believe in organized religion; we believe in organized *relationship* with God the Father through His Son, Jesus Christ. We are not about tradition, but the liberating Word of God. We are not about enduring life—we are about enjoying life!

For more information, please visit joychurch.net